CULINARY FUNGI MAKING SIMPLIFIED

Disclosing the World of Gourmet Mushrooms

JULIAN BENNETT

Table of Contents

CHAPTER ONE

CULINARY FUNGI

Disclosing the World of Gourmet Mushrooms

Mushrooms of a higher culinary quality have become increasingly popular in restaurants around the world. Their unconventional forms, flavors, and aromas make them exciting additions to dishes. While many varieties of gourmet mushrooms are suitable for small-scale cultivation, others can only be collected in the wild.

Find out what gourmet mushrooms are, where to get them, and how to prepare them in this brief introduction.

CHAPTER TWO

Define a gourmet mushroom, please.

Mushrooms are a type of fungus. Mushrooms are the fruiting bodies of fungi, the reproductive structures that disperse the organism's spores. Mycelium, the fungal organism's vegetative part, is typically found either below ground or winding through decomposing matter. However, we are not here to discuss the biology of fungi, but rather the delicious varieties of edible mushrooms.

The most common edible mushroom in the world is the common white mushroom, also known as the crimini mushroom. Those are the ones typically sold in the supermarket's little styrofoam containers. Since they are either not aware of or unable to obtain the more exotic gourmet mushrooms, many people have only ever eaten white mushrooms. Popular gourmet mushrooms range from the relatively common to the extremely rare. Some are extremely rare in comparison to more common ones, making them prohibitively expensive. Check out this rundown of some of the most sought-after gourmet mushrooms and the dishes that best showcase their flavor!

Mushrooms, both oyster and shiitake

The oyster mushroom and the shiitake mushroom share a lot of similarities in their cultivation, but they have very different flavors. They are also some of the most widely available gourmet mushrooms. The oyster and shiitake mushrooms are both found naturally on rotting wood in the forest, but can also be easily cultivated in sterile environments. Farmers of all sizes can maximize their harvests by cultivating them indoors in bags, where they have complete control over the climate. They're so simple to grow that you can even do it in a garage or a spare room at home. Small-scale production of these mushrooms can be quite lucrative due to high demand from local restaurants. Anybody, from serious farmers to weekend warriors, can cash in on the mushroom market by selling their wares to area eateries and supermarkets. Numerous kits are available for purchase, making it simple to begin cultivating your own oyster or shiitake mushrooms at home.

The flavor of oyster mushrooms and shiitake mushrooms is very different. The flavor of oyster mushrooms is reminiscent of shellfish, though it is actually more peppery and earthy. Because of their sturdy consistency, stews and other slow-cooked meals benefit greatly from using them. The tough, dark caps and meaty taste of shiitake mushrooms have made them famous. The stems are inedible, but the caps are delicious and can be used as a standalone food item or as a star in stir-fries and other oven-roasted dishes.

In addition to oyster mushrooms, shiitake, and blewit, many other gourmet varieties are cultivated. All of them are delicious in their own ways and special in their own ways. Since growing most types of gourmet mushrooms is extremely difficult, they are typically harvested from the wild.

Truffle Mushrooms

Mushroom hunting is a common pastime due to the abundance of high-quality gourmet mushrooms that can be found in the wild. While most people who seek out wild mushrooms do so for personal consumption, a few actually collect enough to sell to grocery stores or restaurants. Whatever the case may be, a huge variety of wild mushrooms is collected each year. This is merely a sample.

IMPORTANT: Many gourmet mushrooms have extremely poisonous lookalikes. You should really know what you're doing if you want to go mushroom hunting on your own. In fact, it's recommended that you bring along a professional mushroom hunter.

Mushrooms with Morels

One of the most sought-after gourmet mushrooms is the morel, often shortened to "morels." Since they are so challenging to cultivate, most people who have a taste for gourmet mushrooms resort to harvesting them from the wild. Seeing as morels only appear on the forest floor in the spring, they are highly sought after. Since they spoil quickly, you can't even pickle or dry them to store them. The distinct flavor of morels is often described as a combination of nuttiness, earthiness, and smoke. In fact, they pack so much flavor that a simple butter-and-oil fry is all it takes to make a delicious side dish. It's not just the rich flavor they bring to a dish; it's also the way their unusual form and texture play off of one another.

Shiitake and Chanterelle Mushrooms

Wild chanterelles are another kind of gourmet mushroom that is highly sought after. Their golden color stands out dramatically against the fallen leaves on the forest floor. They are just as ephemeral as morels, emerging from the ground between midsummer and late autumn. However, unlike morels, chanterelles have been preserved and are now available dried or canned. Fruity and nutty in flavor, they are a wonderful addition to many dishes and complement the vibrant hues. Don't overcook them, or they'll get tough and chewy.

Truffles

As far as gourmet mushrooms go, truffles are up there with the best of them. They're a pain to cultivate, nearly impossible to track down, and quickly lose their heady fragrance. Even so, they are a highly sought-after luxury ingredient that adds an extra level of sophistication to any dish. Truffles, like other types of mushrooms, are the result of a fungal infection. It's important to note that these plants have a purely underground life cycle. Finding buried mushrooms is already difficult, but we humans have such a weak sense of smell that we can't even do it. That's why pigs and dogs are used to sniff out truffles. Once the animal begins to dig, the human knows exactly where to look, and he or she carefully removes the gourmet mushroom from the ground.

Although truffles have long been prized in Italian and French kitchens, these days you can find them in restaurants all over the world. Due to the mushroom's extreme richness and potency, only a small portion of the mushroom is typically used at a time. To use them, chefs typically grate them or slice them very thinly. Truffles can also be processed into an oil or butter for longer shelf life. Truffles are one of the most costly food ingredients in the world due to their scarcity, their rich and decadent flavor, and their short shelf life. White truffles fetch prices of up to several thousand dollars per pound. The best I've ever tasted.

Seven Basic Procedures for Cultivating Gourmet Mushrooms

CHAPTER THREE

FINE DINING MUSHROOM CULTURE BECOMES SIMPLER WITH REPEATED EXPERIENCE IN A SUCCESSFUL METHOD. WHAT CAN WE LEARN FROM THE PRODUCTION OF COMMERCIAL MUSHROOMS?

Consider the seven steps in mushroom cultivation outlined by Tradd Cotter in Organic Mushroom Farming and Mycoremediation. These procedures are universal and can be applied to any of the numerous gourmet mushroom cultivation techniques. Our other blogs cover topics such as cultivating shiitakes on logs, oysters on toilet paper, and wine caps on wood chips. In this article, I will outline the general philosophy underlying any technique for cultivating gourmet mushrooms.

The Press Gets Ready

Successful mushroom cultivation relies heavily on having well-prepared growing medium. Growing the mycelium of the fungus is the first step in mushroom cultivation. Substrate treatment to eliminate competing microorganisms is required, or else freshly-dried material rich in cellulose and/or lignin should be used. Due to this, logs and wood chips can be used without any pretreatment. They are difficult for most microorganisms to digest because of their high lignin and cellulose content. To ensure that the desired mushrooms take root before any outside contaminants do, it is best to use them while they are still young and to insert sterile mycelium of those mushrooms into the log. Mushrooms require a number of specific growing conditions, so many substrates, including straw, sawdust, supplemented sawdust, and compost, need to be treated in some way.

Inoculation

The process of inoculation involves introducing spawn or mycelium into a pre-prepared substrate. Mushroom farmers often refer to seeds as "spawn" instead. Since a mushroom does not follow the same lifecycle as a plant, it is technically a different thing, but it serves the same purpose. Mycelium has grown into and around the spawn. Mycelium will immediately begin to grow through the substrate after the spawn is placed in it. What is being inoculated determines the optimal setting for the inoculation process. Logs, straw, and wood chips are all suitable for doing this in the open air, sans shoes and shirts. It's essential to inoculate in a lab with clean airflow when working with high nutrient material like agar, grain, or supplemented sawdust.

Produce Offspring

The spawn run is my favorite stage. Relax and watch the mycelium do its thing. The sight of mycelium spreading across the substrate is truly fascinating. Very often, a very robust growing tip can be seen, which is actively probing the newly prepared substrate with a mycelial web of varying textures. During the spawn run, the mycelium expands at an exponential rate. Mycelia continue to expand at a breakneck pace, colonizing as much of the newly introduced substrate as possible. If it doesn't run out of food or encounter any competitors, it will continue to expand indefinitely. When all of the substrate has been colonized, we can declare the spawn run successful.

Accumulated Population

Mycelial growth changes when a colony is fully established. At this stage, the mycelium's primary goal is to produce a fruiting body by making the most of its current resources rather than growing them. The mycelium immediately begins feeding on the nutrients of the substrate it has colonized. This process, known as symbiosis, involves the mycelium secreting metabolites into the food source and then absorbing sugars and carbon back into the body to fuel the production of new cells and increased food supplies.

Once the substrate is completely occupied, mushroom fruiting can begin.

Pinning

Next to harvesting and preparing mushrooms for consumption, this is my favorite part of the process. When mycelium begins to form a mushroom, a magical and enchanting transformation takes place. When humidity, oxygen, and light levels are all high, tiny baby mushrooms begin to emerge. Mycelium would grow in the log's dark, high-co2 environment before fruiting in the log's lighter, oxygen-rich surroundings. A major factor to fruiting is spore dispersal and this makes sense to most effectively spread spores the mushroom should be in a place that the spores can easily travel out from. Pinning can be triggered by making holes in a plastic bag, or it can start under the bark of a log, leading to the eventual growth of mushrooms.

Fruiting

There are four main factors to manage during fruiting for optimal fruit quality. Not as important to manage when growing a few mushrooms indoors on a grow kit or outdoors on logs, but still good to know for troubleshooting. Controlling and balancing these four factors requires constant listening and adjusting when growing commercially. Humidity, temperature, light, and carbon dioxide levels are the four variables. The ideal amount of light is just enough to read by, but not so much that it will dry out the mushrooms. In the range of 85 percent humidity and 50 to 75 degrees Fahrenheit, depending on the species (some grow well outside that range). As a general rule, atmospheric concentrations of carbon dioxide (Co2) should be kept below 1,000 parts per million. While oysters are particularly vulnerable to elevated CO2 levels, shiitake, lion's mane, and many other gourmet mushrooms thrive at levels well above 1000 ppm. Those interested in cultivating gourmet mushrooms should not give up too easily if their first few attempts at it are unsuccessful. Bacteria and other fungi are guaranteed to get in the way of your success, but persevere and you will eventually prevail.

Rest

All things require downtime. Fungi, like plants, animals, fish, bacteria, and others, need their nighttime rest. Mushroom fruiting is a difficult process, and the fungus needs time to recover. At this point, the fungi are still consuming the substrate and stocking up on nutrients for the next fruiting. I hope you find this breakdown on growing gourmet mushrooms to be helpful in your quest for abundant mushrooms harvests.

www.ingramcontent.com/pod-product-compliance
Lightning Source LLC
La Vergne TN
LVHW010124170826
845678LV00012B/2582